T0233759

# The Taxobook

*History, Theories, and Concepts of Knowledge Organization*

Part 1 of a 3-Part Series

# Synthesis Lectures on Information Concepts, Retrieval, and Services

Editor

**Gary Marchionini**, *University of North Carolina, Chapel Hill*

Synthesis Lectures on Information Concepts, Retrieval, and Services is edited by Gary Marchionini of the University of North Carolina. The series will publish 50- to 100-page publications on topics pertaining to information science and applications of technology to information discovery, production, distribution, and management. The scope will largely follow the purview of premier information and computer science conferences, such as ASIST, ACM SIGIR, ACM/IEEE JCDL, and ACM CIKM. Potential topics include, but not are limited to: data models, indexing theory and algorithms, classification, information architecture, information economics, privacy and identity, scholarly communication, bibliometrics and webometrics, personal information management, human information behavior, digital libraries, archives and preservation, cultural informatics, information retrieval evaluation, data fusion, relevance feedback, recommendation systems, question answering, natural language processing for retrieval, text summarization, multimedia retrieval, multilingual retrieval, and exploratory search.

The Taxobook: History, Theories, and Concepts of Knowledge Organization: Part 1
Marjorie M.K. Hlava
October 2014

Children's Internet Search: Using Roles to Understand Children's Search Behavior
Elizabeth Foss and Allison Druin
September 2014

Digital Library Technologies: Complex Objects, Annotation, Ontologies, Classification, Extraction, and Security
Edward A. Fox, Ricardo da Silva Torres
March 2014

Digital Libraries Applications: CBIR, Education, Social Networks, eScience/Simulation, and GIS
Edward A. Fox, Jonathan P. Leidig
March 2014

© Springer Nature Switzerland AG 2022

Reprint of original edition © Morgan & Claypool 2015

All rights reserved. No part of this publication may be reproduced, stored in a retrieval system, or transmitted in any form or by any means—electronic, mechanical, photocopy, recording, or any other except for brief quotations in printed reviews, without the prior permission of the publisher.

The Taxobook: History, Theories, and Concepts of Knowledge Organization
Part 1 of a 3-Part Series
Marjorie M.K. Hlava


ISBN: 978-3-031-01159-7  print
ISBN: 978-3-031-02287-6  ebook

DOI 10.1007/978-3-031-02287-6

A Publication in the Springer series
*SYNTHESIS LECTURES ON INFORMATION CONCEPTS, RETRIEVAL, AND SERVICES #35*

Series Editor: Gary Marchionini, University of North Carolina, Chapel Hill

Series ISSN 1947-945X Print    1947-9468 Electronic

# The Taxobook

*History, Theories, and Concepts of*
*Knowledge Organization*

Part 1 of a 3-Part Series

**Marjorie M.K. Hlava**
Access Innovations, Inc., Albuquerque, New Mexico

*SYNTHESIS LECTURES ON INFORMATION CONCEPTS, RETRIEVAL,*
*AND SERVICES #35*

# ABSTRACT

This is the first volume in a series about creating and maintaining taxonomies and their practical applications, especially in search functions.

In Book 1 (*The Taxobook: History, Theories, and Concepts of Knowledge Organization*), the author introduces the very foundations of classification, starting with the ancient Greek philosophers Plato and Aristotle, as well as Theophrastus and the Roman Pliny the Elder. They were first in a line of distinguished thinkers and philosophers to ponder the organization of the world around them and attempt to apply a structure or framework to that world.

The author continues by discussing the works and theories of several other philosophers from Medieval and Renaissance times, including Saints Aquinas and Augustine, William of Occam, Andrea Cesalpino, Carl Linnaeus, and René Descartes.

In the 17th, 18th, and 19th centuries, John Locke, Immanuel Kant, James Frederick Ferrier, Charles Ammi Cutter, and Melvil Dewey contributed greatly to the theories of classification systems and knowledge organization. Cutter and Dewey, especially, created systems that are still in use today.

Chapter 8 covers the contributions of Shiyali Ramamrita Ranganathan, who is considered by many to be the "father of modern library science." He created the concept of faceted vocabularies, which are widely used—even if they are not well understood—on many e-commerce websites.

Following the discussions and historical review, the author has included a glossary that covers all three books of this series so that it can be referenced as you work your way through the second and third volumes. The author believes that it is important to understand the history of knowledge organization and the differing viewpoints of various philosophers—even if that understanding is only that the differing viewpoints simply exist. Knowing the differing viewpoints will help answer the fundamental questions: Why do we want to build taxonomies? How do we build them to serve multiple points of view?

## KEYWORDS

taxonomy, thesaurus, controlled vocabulary, search, retrieval, ontology, knowledge organization, classification, theory of knowledge, semantics, knowledge management, library science, information science

# Contents

This book is dedicated to all taxonomists, past, present, and future. My team at Access Innovations worked hard and long to bring this book to fruition. It would not have been done without their encouragement, patience, and support.

# List of Figures

# Preface

Most of us are keenly—personally—aware that over the past several years, information on the Internet has been rapidly expanding, with a flood of information pouring out of computer screens to people everywhere. In 1998, Google reported 3.6 million searches for the year. In 2012, they reported an average of over 5 billion searches every day. That's an increase of over 52 million percent! They claim 67% of the search market, so there remains another 33% of the market of searches to add to that 5 billion.

We use search often. We use search so often that "Google" has become a verb, at least in practice. "Google it" has become an everyday phrase. Early in my career, searching the Internet (or its precursor, DARPAnet) was the purview of professionals with special training, special access, and special equipment. We were an elite group of gatekeepers, in a way, with access to a corpus of knowledge desirable to researchers but inaccessible except through professional searchers.

In response to our search queries—when we "just Google" something—the search engines like Google, Yahoo, Ask, and others return billions of hits within milliseconds, but how many of those billions of hits does the searcher actually need… or want? How often do you find that the site you seek is at the top of the search results page? How often do you find that the search results don't include what you seek, or that it is buried 10 pages down? How often do you look through 10 pages of search results to see if your desired site is listed at all? How do we contend with this exploding flood of information and find what we actually need? Search needs help!

A parallel expansion—or explosion—has been occurring in intranets, where individual organizational and enterprise information resides. Organizations are eagerly adopting technologies that can locate and sort out the information that is wanted and needed. In this environment, as Jean Graef of the Montague Institute put it shortly after the turn of the millennium, "Taxonomies have recently emerged from the quiet backwaters of biology, book indexing, and library science into the corporate limelight." Corporate librarians, information technology specialists, and others involved in information storage and retrieval recognize and acknowledge the value of taxonomies. However, these people often lack an understanding of taxonomies and of how they are created, maintained and implemented.

In response we have developed this guide to taxonomy creation, development, maintenance, and implementation. We will progress rapidly from theory to practice because both are critical for a comprehensive knowledge. The guide is intended to cover the full spectrum from the original scoping of the work through its use in tagging (indexing with keywords from the taxonomy), web site navigation, search, author and affiliation/organization disambiguation, identification of peer reviewers, recommendation systems, data mashups, and a myriad of other applications.

In this volume, I explore the philosophical and theoretical foundations of classification, highlighting the contributions of individuals who sought to understand the world around them by applying order to that world. These thinkers go back to ancient Greek and Roman times, and include such outstanding philosophers as Aristotle, Plato, Theophrastus, and Pliny the Elder. This exploration continues with the insights of later writers, including Thomas Aquinas, Augustine of Hippo, William of Occam, Andrea Cesalpino, Carl Linnaeus, René Descartes, John Locke, Immanuel Kant, James Frederick, Charles Ammi Cutter, Melvil Dewey, and Shiyali Ramanrita Ranganathan.

It is my hope that this historical exploration will provide an effective background for a deeper understanding of knowledge organization. While the writers who are discussed had some disagreements, even those disagreements might serve to highlight some awareness of issues of which taxonomists should be aware, especially one fundamental one: Why do we want to build taxonomies?

In Book 2 (*The Taxobook: Principles and Practices of Building Taxonomies*) I suggest reasons for creating a taxonomy and how it can be used to advantage in an organization. I present and describe various forms of controlled vocabularies, including taxonomies, thesauri, and ontologies, and include methods for constructing taxonomies—or other kinds of controlled vocabularies. Standards, especially information standards, are near and dear to my heart, and I have served on several committees and review boards for many of the information standards published by NISO and other standards-forming organizations. Therefore the last chapter of Book 2 provides an abbreviated list of the specific standards that I feel are most important to knowledge and information professionals, brief descriptions of some of the standards forming organizations, and the process that they go through in creating these standards or guidelines. While standards might sound like a dry subject best used to cure insomnia, I suggest that they will provide you with an excellent framework for your taxonomy construction project.

Book 3 (*The Taxobook: Applications, Implementations, and Integration in Search*), then, covers putting your taxonomy into use. It's all well and good to create a beautiful taxonomy that classifies The World As We Know It, that conforms to all of the appropriate standards, and is practically perfect in every way, but what good does it do? In order to get back your investment, you have to integrate your taxonomy into whatever workflow or system your organization employs. In Book 3 we discuss the various ways in which you can apply, implement, and integrate your taxonomy into that workflow, with an emphasis on integrating a taxonomy into search. Lastly, I ponder the future of knowledge management. I don't know exactly where we are going, but I have some good guesses based on where we have been and the trends I see in requests from my clients. Based on my guesses, I provide a few suggestions about areas in which you might start to prepare.

While I can't truly predict the future, I am quite certain that the volume of information coming at us isn't going to go away, lessen in intensity, or slow down. The information explosion is going to continue, and we all need to find ways to make sense of it—to improve retrieval, to refine analysis, to pull out the real value of information so that the people who need it, get it.

I hope that you will find this series practical and useful, and perhaps these volumes will become part of your desktop reference collection. Throughout this series, I attempt to include information that will help you to make a business case for your taxonomy construction project, as well as simple to use, step-by-step instructions for creating a taxonomy and leveraging it in multiple ways throughout your organization.

# Acknowledgments

The series started as a series of talks and lectures given to various groups as full-day workshops on how to build and implement thesauri, controlled vocabularies, and databases. The audiences helped hone the message and poked holes in my assertions when appropriate. This was combined with over 600 engagements over the years with fascinating clients who each needed a similar endpoint but with a unique twist because of their content and their individual visions. These combined with the need to educate staff members in how the work is done and creation of best practices as well as broad support on the standards bodies to create an unusual perspective on the knowledge organization and distribution process.

This work would not be possible without the tireless efforts and uncompromising support of many, many, people. My business partner and friend for most of my professional life, Jay Ven Eman, has been unstinting in his support and encouragement, although he does occasionally roll his eyes at some of my ideas. The team at Access Innovations reviewed the drafts and, in particular, Heather Kotula, Barbara Gilles, Tim Soholt, and David (Win) Hansen, who massaged the draft, untangled my prose, improved the images and examples, and offered very pertinent suggestions to create the final product. Our customers who provided the content and allowed us to work with it have provided an unparalleled laboratory of material for organization to meet their individual needs. To my own family for their cheerful understanding and putting up with the demands of career and writing, my husband Paul Hlava, my daughters Heather and Holly and their families. And to my Mom, Mary Kimmel, who showed me that you can have a career and a happy family too.

Many people encouraged me to write down what I was teaching and I am grateful for their continued insistence. Tim Lamkins for his early review and insightful comments, Clients whose works we reference in case studies and examples, and my industry mentors including Roger Summit, Eugene Garfield, Buzzy Basch, Tom Hogan, and Kate Noerr.

To all of these and more I thank you; I could not have done this without you!
Marjorie M.K. Hlava

CHAPTER 1

# Origins of Knowledge Organization Theory: Early Philosophy of Knowledge

At their core, rigorous classification frameworks represent ways of organizing and managing knowledge. You could even say that taxonomies and thesauri exist to *further the objective* of organizing knowledge. Exploring the historical background of knowledge organization will help us gain a better understanding of these essential information systems.

Formal taxonomy has roots in the musings of ancient Greek philosophers, and their innovative thinking is an excellent place to begin the discussion of knowledge theory, to spark the fire of creative visualization, unifying words and mental constructs.

What is knowledge? Plato 428–347 BC, a pre-eminent philosophical thinker during the Golden Age of Greece, [1] defined knowledge as "justified true belief." On the other hand, and possibly reflecting the increased complexities and uncertainties of his time, 20th-century writer Bertrand Russell raised the following reservations, with regard to pinpointing the nature of truth (knowledge):

> "...at first sight it might be thought that knowledge might be defined as belief which is in agreement with the facts. The trouble is that no one knows what a belief is, no one knows what a fact is, and no one knows what sort of agreement between them would make a belief true." [2]

With roots in ancient Greece, Platonic realism linked knowledge with the perception of observable "reality." If we dare risk simplifying his theoretical stance, we could agree that Plato held firmly the assertion that *knowing reality* is what philosophy is all about. In Plato's time, a person with an inquisitive mind, desiring to learn more about reality, and thus, increase his own knowledge—to use the Greek, *gnosis*—might seek teachers who would expose him to "philosophy" as a whole. In Classical Greece, philosophy encompassed the fields of Western knowledge, including some disciplines we still think of as philosophy today (logic, metaphysics, theology, and ethics) and others we would now usually categorize as major divisions of the "hard sciences" (e.g., physics, biology, and mathematics). Entirely new intellectual disciplines have sprouted up since the Greek categorizations. Dramatic evolutions have been seen within longstanding knowledge traditions, even within academic fields regarded at one time or another as already solidified, or solidifying, into their final, organized forms. Back then, a curious individual would not, as we are predisposed to do in modern times, narrow his interests almost immediately into a specialized branch of study.

Since the synthesis of early modern philosophy in the late Renaissance, Western philosophy has generally been regarded as pertaining to analytically rigorous methods for examining aspects of metaphysics, epistemology, ethics, aesthetics, and logic. Scholars invoke the word "philosophy" when discussing the elegant, formal, narrative descriptions that often resulted when a talented thinker focused his concentration and deliberation on a subject of intellectual analysis.

Scientific inquiry into nature, abstract mathematics, and the like developed into self-defining and, to some degree, self-organizing academic domains. Plato and his contemporaries loosely bundled these areas of intellectual investigation, which we would usually see as belonging to separate realms, under one blanket concept: "knowledge."

As a former botanist, I am pleased to defer to another plant classification specialist, the eminent Dr. Tod Stuessy, to explain what happened next during the transition to our modern ways of thinking regarding structured vocabularies:

> "To gain a full understanding of the progression of species concepts... we need to turn first to the philosophers of the Greek civilization, and particularly to Plato. Plato's philosophy dealt in part with the organization of all things and contained the concept of the **eidos** or "species" to refer to any different kind of thing. All objects were considered as being only shadows of the **eidos**, and consequently, variation was overlooked in favor of the **typological species** approach that would develop greater biological proportions under Aristotle...
>
> The principle of logical division used by Aristotle, based in part upon the ideas of Plato, was to be the basis of taxonomy for many years to come, and it served as a schema upon which his species concept was framed. According to the principles of logical division, a species was any unit possessing a common essence (i.e., an abstract idea or concept that makes the unit what it is), and this logical species was a relative term, being applicable to various levels in a classification scheme. A logical relationship existed between the genus and species, this connection being determined by the use of the **species differentia** and a **fundamendum divisionis** that was both mutually exclusive and exhaustive. Consequently, a species was defined on an a priori basis and was regarded as fixed and unchanging." [3]

During Aristotle's time (he lived from 384–322 BC), the goal of systematically organizing information became firmly established as a means for expanding the reach of empirical evidence. As he was a student of Plato, it was perhaps natural that Aristotle should expand on Platonic approaches to the methodical classification of knowledge.

Figure 1.1: "Sanzio 01," by Raphael, featuring Plato and Aristotle beneath the central arch of the School of Athens—Stitched together from vatican.va.

Aristotle's *History of Animals* classified a large set of organisms, each in relation to a hierarchical "Ladder of Life" (*scala naturae*). This very early example of a wide-scale information classification scheme included hierarchical arrangements and set the pattern for biological taxonomies for subsequent millennia. He included hierarchy levels representing animal *genera* and *species* and incorporated the distinction between organisms with vertebrate skeletons from those that are invertebrates.

Aristotle's substantial accomplishments in classifying the names of living things were carried on by a colleague, Theophrastus (371–287 BC). Later, when the locus of rational activities shifted to Rome, Pliny the Elder (23–79 AD) classified numerous plants, using binomial (two-part) names in portions of his scheme.

CHAPTER 2

# Saints and Traits: Realism and Nominalism

Neo-Platonic realism, linking knowledge with observation, was extended by Saint Augustine (354–430 AD) and by Saint Thomas Aquinas (1225–1274).

Figure 2.2: Portrait of Saint Augustine by Phillippe de Champaigne.

Figure 2.3: Saint Thomas Aquinas, from "Gentile da Fabriano 052," by Gentile da Fabriano.

Saints Augustine and Aquinas provided important advancements in taxonomic thinking with the realizations that (1) an object's *characteristic traits* define its nature, plus (2) characteristics define the classes to which objects belong. That is to say, two objects with wholly divergent characteristics cannot reasonably be thought of as belonging in a category that, otherwise, houses objects of the same kind. Basically, they frowned on mixing similar and dissimilar things.

> *"Realism, at its simplest and most general, is the view that entities of a certain type have an objective reality, a reality that is completely ontologically independent of our conceptual schemes, linguistic practices, beliefs, etc. Thus, entities (including abstract concepts and universals as well as more concrete objects) have an existence independent of the act of perception, and independent of their names."* [4]

This line of philosophic thinking has spanned centuries. Legions of philosophers and great thinkers have debated these concepts, some to their serious detriment (exile, excommunication, and death), and attempting to fully explain these schools of thought is far beyond the scope of this book. However, the following summarization may be helpful:

> *"**Realism** is contrasted with **Anti-Realism** (any position **denying** the objective reality of entities) and with **Nominalism** (the position that abstract concepts, general terms or universals have **no independent existence**, but exist only as **names**) and with **Idealism** (the position that the mind is all that exists, and that the **external world** is an **illusion** created by the mind)."* [5]

Figure 2.3: "William of Ockham," reconstructed from a public domain source by Moscarlop—own work.

As the drama of knowledge theory unfolds in the next act, center stage is occupied by William of Ockham (c. 1287–1347) [6], an English friar and philosopher, whose perspective on shared characteristics was a bit different than the orientation described above.

> *"Ockham was a nominalist, indeed he is the person whose name is perhaps most famously associated with nominalism. But nominalism means many different things:*

- *A denial of metaphysical universals. Ockham was emphatically a nominalist in this sense.*

- *An emphasis on reducing one's ontology to a bare minimum, on paring down the supply of fundamental ontological categories. Ockham was likewise a nominalist in this sense.*

- *A denial of 'abstract' entities. Depending on what one means, Ockham was or was not a nominalist in this sense. He believed in 'abstractions' such as **whiteness** and **humanity**, for instance, although he did not believe they were universals. (On the contrary, there are at least as many distinct **whitenesses** as there are **white things**.) He certainly believed in immaterial entities such as God and angels. He did not believe in mathematical ("quantitative") entities of any kind.*

*The first two kinds of nominalism listed above are independent of one another. Historically, there have been philosophers who denied metaphysical universals, but allowed (individual) entities in more ontological categories than Ockham does. Conversely, one might reduce the number of ontological categories, and yet hold that universal entities are needed in the categories that remain."* [7]

To use another example, the Wikipedia article about nominalism explains it by focusing on the single characteristic of greenness that unites different things into a single category:

*"One wants to know in virtue of what are Fluffy and Kitzler both cats and what makes the grass, the shirt, and Kermit green. The realist answer is that all the green things are green in virtue of the existence of a universal; a single abstract thing, in this case, that is a part of all the green things. With respect to the color of the grass, the shirt and Kermit, one of their parts is identical. In this respect, the three parts are literally one. Greenness is repeatable because there is one thing that manifests itself wherever there are green things."*

**Felinity—represented by cats**

** Fluffy

Figure 2.4: Fluffy, a cat. By Alvesgaspar.

** Kitzler

Figure 2.5: Kitzler, a cat. By Hisashi.

**Greenness—represented by green things**

* * Grass

Figure 2.6: "Grass dsc08672-nevit,"
by Nevit Dilmen.

** Green Shirt

Figure 2.7: "Opium für's Ohr 07,"
by Krd—own work.

* * Green leaves

Figure 2.8: Green Leaves, by Petr Kratochvil.

Although Ockham is credited with being a nominalist [8], he actually ended up occupying a position somewhere in the middle between realism and nominalism. By maintaining that universal distinctions exist as general concepts, rather than as rigid controls, he broke through the strict nominalist orientation, to conclude correctly that categories and object classes are, in fact, dependent upon our minds.

Because mental constructs are informed by extracting subtle details and fine qualities from our individual experiences, he realized that, as a result, there will always be variations in categorization, by necessity, based on interpretations. And, also, there will be variations in category from differences with extrapolating existing concepts for application in the naming and sorting of novel objects or ideas.

Ockham's contribution can be boiled down to differentiating between an *object* or *concept* vs. what we *perceive* or *know* vs. *what we call it*. Applied to our taxonomy work, this means we each may view the world differently but must come to some agreement about using commonly recognized names for things—which is really the basis for controlled vocabulary.

CHAPTER   3

# Arranging the Flowers... and the Birds, and the Insects, and Everything Else: Early Naturalists and Taxonomies

Now we jump to Italy in the 16th century. Philosopher and botanist Andrea Cesalpino (1519–1603) is sometimes referred to as "the first taxonomist," largely because of his classification of plant species, De Plantis. First printed in 1583, this catalog of plant species is regarded as the first substantive textbook for teaching botany. Cesalpino sorted the plant species into various plant families—including one large family group of sunflowers, daisies, and asters, and another large family group containing mustard, broccoli, cabbages, and cauliflower. Those two plant families from the Renaissance era were retained as valid classifications in modern botany.

Figure 3.1: "Andrea Cesalpino."

In the 17th century, English naturalist John Ray made significant contributions to the art and science of developing taxonomies. These contributions are still recognized not just by botanists, but also by scientists in fields such as astronomy and geology who are interested in classification:

> *"The seeds for classification lie in the works of the British naturalist John Ray (1628–1705). ....*
> *Ray classified plants by overall morphology: the classification in his 1682 book* Methodus Plantarum Nova *draws on flowers, seeds, fruits, and roots. ... This method produced more "natural" results than "artificial" systems based on one feature alone (such as "greenness"; it expressed the similarities between species more fully."* ...

*"And so, too, it is with galaxies. Each is unique in its own right, no less than each snowflake or every seashell; although each has a unique form, it is the challenge of the morphologist to group these into form families."* [9]

One of the interesting things about Mr. Ray's work is that until his time, all naturalists had been using the natural order for their main orientation toward classifying—that is, things of the sea were placed together in a conceptual framework, things of the forest were grouped together, and so on, throughout the wild realms of nature. Beginning with Ray and continuing with Linnaeus, naturalists relied on the actual morphology of the plant or animal itself, when attempting to classify new organisms. These taxonomists conceived frameworks in which the information about where a plant or creature lived was irrelevant for the purpose of categorizing its species. Progress toward identifying what are the essential defining characteristics of a thing is a challenge that continues for modern taxonomists—in biology and in the information science sphere.

In Western Europe, the 18th century witnessed more advances in classification practices, especially from the mind of Carl Linnaeus (1707–1778), a Swedish zoologist and botanist, who is often regarded as the "father of modern taxonomy."

Figure 3.2: "Carolus Linnaeus by Hendrik Hollander 1853," by Hendrik Hollander, University of Amsterdam.

Contrary to popular belief, Carl Linnaeus did not invent the modern binomial nomenclature system, with organism types that are designated by genus and species. That particular honor belongs to the Bauhin brothers, Gaspard (1560–1624) (alternately, "Gaspar" or "Caspar"), and Johann

("Jean") (1541–1613). [10] These creative Swiss brothers formalized a method that was reliant upon polynomial nomenclature—often vague and wordy—and introduced a stricter, more logical naming convention with one word representing the genus and one word indicating the species, for productive combinations, with the discovery of new animals and plants.

The Bauhin brothers did not *consistently* apply binomial nomenclature in their taxonomic efforts, whereas Linnaeus did so. Moreover, Linnaeus employed a more scientific and consistent approach, applying numerous rules and principles to ensure qualities of taxonomic orderliness. This approach included guidelines for such tricky issues as: (a) correctly indicating synonyms; (b) maintaining clarity and succinctness of terminology; and (c) precluding any use of words representing *the abstract other*, such as "anonymous" or (as we occasionally see in taxonomy development projects), the useless and confusing modifier "other." Many of Linnaeus' guidelines are central to our modern information technology work.

T. A. Sprague summarizes:

> "Linnaeus was, first and foremost, a systematist, whose aim was to bring order out of chaos in the classification of living organisms. . . . Descriptions of the individual genera were supplied in the successive editions of his "Genera Plantarum," and diagnoses [differentiating descriptions; cf. definitions and scope notes] of the species with their principal synonyms in his "Species Plantarum." In order that these descriptions and diagnoses might be clearly intelligible, he provided a system of terminology applicable to the various morphological categories recognized by him. Finally, for convenience of reference, he selected a name, old or new, for each of the genera upheld by him, and in 1753, a true binary name … for each of his species, designed to replace the often cumbrous diagnostic phrases under which they had previously passed." [11]

As a naturalist, Carl Linnaeus had the knowledge to place individual species in the various categories, or genera, that he devised or adopted from previous naturalists' works. Many of his groupings are still recognized by botanists and zoologists. Conceptualizing on the broadest scale, he systematized the very kingdoms of nature in his *Systema Naturae*, in the form of the animal/vegetable/mineral scheme that remains familiar to this day. The full title of Linnaeus' major work can be translated as "System of nature through the three kingdoms of nature, according to classes, orders, genera and species, with characters, differences, synonyms, places." This was a true and comprehensive taxonomic hierarchy—containing nested hierarchies and some other characteristics that are specific to thesauri, as we will discuss in later chapters.

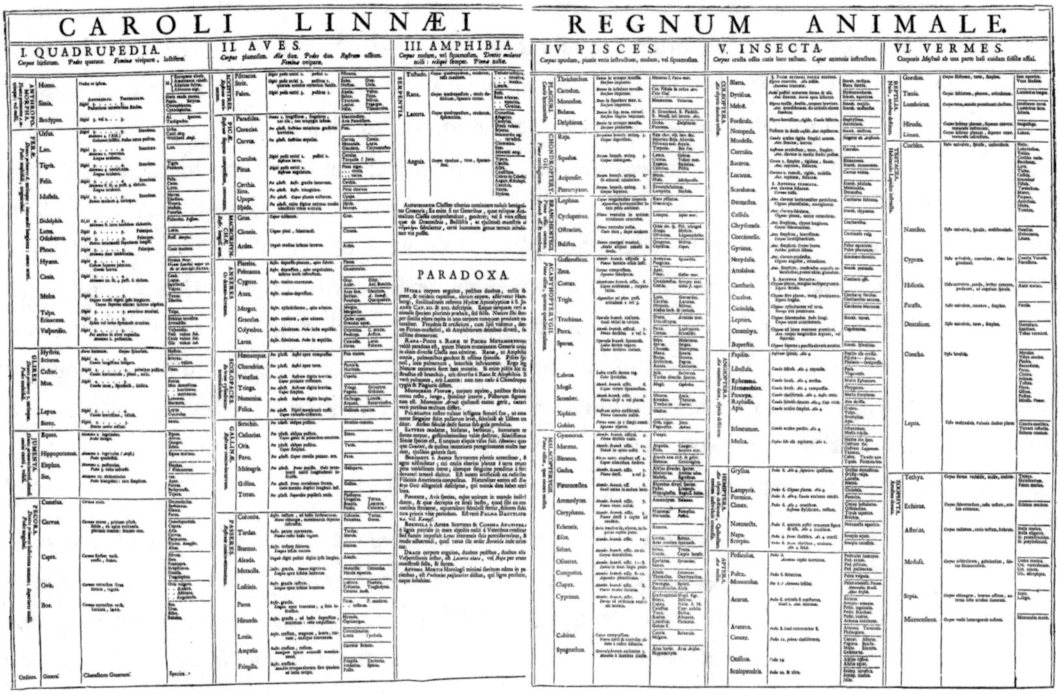

Figure 3.3: "Linnaeus: Regnum Animale (1735)."

CHAPTER 4

# The Age of Enlightenment Impacts Knowledge Theory

In the 17th century, the picture of knowledge theory was impacted by Enlightenment thinking. René Descartes (1596–1650), first of the century's rationalist thinkers, studied epistemology—the nature of knowledge—among many other subject areas, and he wrote his arguments in exquisite, granular, logical steps. He is perhaps best known as the philosopher who proclaimed in the Latin, "*Cogito ergo sum*"—"I think, therefore I exist." As a mathematician, Descartes established equations and principles capturing critical nuances of advances in modern algebra and symbolic logic.

Figure 4.1: "Frans Hals: Portret van René Descartes," after Frans Hals (1582/1583–1666): André Hatala [e.a.] (1997), De eeuw van Rembrandt, Bruxelles.

Of particular interest to any taxonomist is Descartes' famous Wax Argument. In opposition to some of the arguments put forth by Aristotle, Plato, Saints Augustine and Aquinas, and Ockham,

Descartes posits that to classify something only according to its apparent characteristics is a questionable approach. He considered a piece of wax, which changes as it becomes warm. Think about it. The candle, a solid object, slowly becomes more a liquid as it is heated. So which is it—solid or liquid? Descartes used the Wax Argument to support his position that perception is unreliable, and that it changes with passing conditions such as time or temperature. Descartes argued that human beings truly acquire knowledge better through deductive reasoning than through observation.

Figure 4.2: Candle burning by Matthew Bowden.

The next grand figure on the epistemology stage is John Locke (1632–1704), an English physician who broke new philosophical ground.

Figure 4.3: "John Locke," by Sir Godfrey Kneller: State Hermitage Museum, St. Petersburg, Russia.

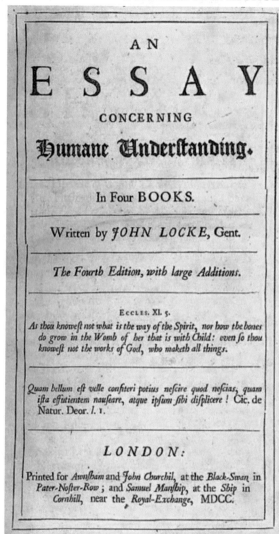

AN

E S S A Y

CONCERNING

Humane Understanding.

In Four BOOKS.

Written by *JOHN LOCKE*, Gent.

*The Fourth Edition, with large Additions.*

ECCLES. XI. 5.

As thou knoweft not what is the way of the Spirit, nor how the bones do grow in the Womb of her that is with Child: even fo thou knoweft not the works of God, who maketh all things.

Quam bellum eft velle confiteri potius nefcire quod nefcias, quam ifta effutientem naufeare, atque ipfum fibi difplicere ! Cic. de Natur. Deor. *l.* 1.

LONDON:

Printed for *Awnfham* and *John Churchil*, at the *Black-Swan* in *Pater-Nofter-Row* ; and *Samuel Manfhip*, at the *Ship* in *Cornhill*, near the *Royal-Exchange*, MDCC.

Figure 4.4: "Locke Essay," by John Locke (1632–1704): Locke, John. An essay concerning human understanding. 4th ed. London Printed for Awnsham and John Churchil, and Samuel Manship, 1700. University of Sydney, Rare Books Library.

In *An Essay Concerning Human Understanding*, he maintained that, at birth, the human mind is a blank slate, and that all knowledge is acquired through perception and experience.

Locke identified three kinds of knowledge, differing both in the way the knowledge is acquired and in the degree of certainty they provide:

- **intuitive knowledge** provides the highest degree of certainty,

- **demonstrative knowledge** provides less certainty, and

- **sensitive knowledge** provides the lowest degree of certainty, which can be thought of as probability.

Book III of the essay explores the relationships between words and concepts, an area of particular interest in connection with controlled vocabularies. As for classification, and for biological taxonomy in particular, Locke starts from the old idea of "essences." In the quote below, he comments on the relationship between classification and characteristics, and on the arbitrariness that is sometimes unavoidable in classification:

> "Academic wrangling about genus and species has had the effect of almost entirely suppressing that original meaning of 'essence.' Instead of referring to the real constitutions of things, essences these days are usually thought of in a second way, in which they are connected with the artificial constitution of genus and species. Real constitutions are ones that are laid down in the things themselves; artificial ones are products of human artifice, that is, of human classificatory procedures."

Locke goes on to reject nominalism:

> "Nominal essences are tied to names. Whether a given thing x is to be described by a given general name depends purely on whether x has the essence that makes it conform to the abstract idea that the name is associated with." [12]

We consider Descartes and Locke to be enlightened relative to their predecessors, and they made major contributions to our modern concept of taxonomy. They laid much of the groundwork for the basis of Western thought, the way we think and the basis for taxonomies today.

Figure 4.5: From "Etymology of taxonomy" search on Google.

CHAPTER 5

# 18th-Century Developments: Knowledge Theory Coming to the Foreground

Like the preceding century, the 18th century also brought changes in the philosophy of knowledge. One highly influential writer was the Prussian philosopher Immanuel Kant (1724–1804).

Figure 5.1: "Immanuel Kant (painted portrait)," by unspecified: /History/Carnegie/kant/portrait.html.

Kant's major work was the *Critique of Pure Reason*, first published in 1781. Kant discusses the nature of *a priori* and *a posteriori* judgments and concepts, challenging earlier philosophical writings on the subject. Roughly speaking, *a priori* knowledge is knowledge that is known independently of experience; it is non-empirical, or arrived at beforehand, usually by reason. In contrast, *a posteriori* knowledge is knowledge that is known by experience; it is empirical, or arrived at after experience and observation.

*"In simple terms, Kant argued that our experiences are structured by necessary features of our minds. The mind shapes and structures experience so that, on an abstract level, all human experience shares certain essential structural features. Among other things, Kant believed that the concepts of **space** and **time** are integral to all human experience, as are our concepts of **cause** and **effect**. We never have direct experience of things, the **phenomenal** world, and what we do experience is the phenomenal world as conveyed by our **senses**."* [13]

This is Kant's way of expressing the importance of individual perception from "knowing" the world and nature. The diagram below illustrates Kant's theory of perception, as explained in the *Critique of Pure Reason*.

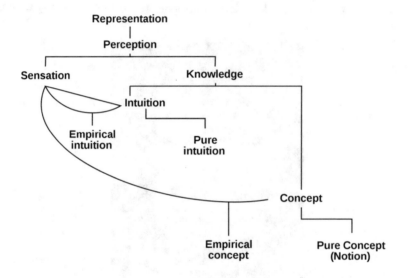

Figure 5.2: By B. Jankuloski (vectorisation). Original by Lucidish.

As Carl Linnaeus presented the world with a taxonomy of nature, Kant presented the world with a taxonomy of knowledge, delineating how analytical judgments contain our predicate concepts within their subjects: how human categories positively structure our views on nature, and its laws.

A taxonomist might wonder to which element a taxonomy term applies. Together they drive home the point of "aboutness" in the creation of any outline of knowledge like a taxonomy. Language is not exact but it is used to describe concepts often using parallel concepts to expand the explanation. Without these comparisons we don't have a frame of reference.

# CHAPTER 6

# High Resolution: Classification Sharpens in the 19th and 20th Centuries

In the 19th century, the study of the nature of knowledge came to be known as epistemology. The term was introduced by Scottish metaphysicist James Frederick Ferrier (1808–1864).

Figure 6.1: "James Frederick Ferrier," by Unknown: Scan from website.

Epistemological writers explored how knowledge relates to connected notions, such as belief and truth—and perception, as discussed by Immanuel Kant. They also considered the means of producing knowledge. And to a large extent, they embraced skepticism, a mode of thinking requiring information to be well supported by evidence before being accepted as fact, i.e., knowledge.

Here we see how philosophy and science were developing hand-in-hand. This continued into the 20th century. The study of knowledge broadened in response to key contributions from psychology (especially in the areas of memory and perception), library science, linguistics, and computer science. Information science became a separate field, covering such things as linguistic analysis and vocabulary control.

Speaking of library science, let's revisit the 19th century, when the rise of classification occurred. As far as this author is concerned, the hero of classification systems is Charles Ammi Cutter (1837–1903).

Figure 6.2: Charles Ammi Cutter. By Boston Athenaeum.

As a librarian at Harvard College, Mr. Cutter invented the card catalog, using an author index and a "class catalog," or subject index. Previously, library holdings were usually listed in published books, large and unwieldy for actual use by a researcher. In Cutter's methods, the beginnings of modern approaches to subject matter classification can be discerned.

Later, influenced by the decimal system of Melvil Dewey, Cutter came up with the Cutter Expansive Classification system. This library system described seven levels of classification, utilizing each level to achieve increasing specificity.

According to library historian Leo E. LaMontagne, "Cutter produced the best classification of the nineteenth century. [Its] key features—notation, specificity, and versatility—make it deserving of the praise it has received." Unfortunately, Charles Cutter died before he could finish his classification system. It is still used by many small libraries, and it served as a foundation for the Library of Congress subject headings.

Proof that Cutter was a forward-looking thinker can be found in his prescient article, "The Boston Public Library in 1983," published one hundred years before. Here's one of the remarkable predictions in the article:

> "The desks had every convenience that could facilitate study; but what most caught my eye was a little key-board at each, connected by a wire with the librarian's desk. The reader had only to find the mark of his book in the catalog, touch a few lettered or numbered keys, and on the instant a runner at the central desk started for the volume, and, appearing after an astonishingly short interval at the door nearest his desk, brought him his book and took his acknowledgment without disturbing any of the neighboring readers."

Of course, no text about the history of classification theory can exclude mention of Melvil Dewey (1851–1931), inventor of the Dewey Decimal Classification system (or, if you prefer, DDC, or the Dewey Decimal System).

Figure 6.3: "Melvil Dewey."

Most readers are already familiar with the DDC, or they might know of the Universal Decimal Classification, which is based on the DDC.

What's so great about the DDC? Someone asked that very question in 2006. The query continued,

> "It seems obvious that if you have to categorize a huge number of objects (say, books for example), you would set up a set of unique categories, sort the objects into the appropriate category, and then itemize the objects within that category. Is Dewey famous just because it's the standard, or is there more to the system that makes it so great?"

Dex, of The Straight Dope, answered, in part:

> "What's obvious to you, the jaded library patron, wasn't so obvious in the era before Melvil Dewey. Once a creative genius comes up with an innovation, a century later everyone thinks it's obvious. If you think it's so easy, you come up with a system for classifying all knowledge that ever was and ever will be."

Of course Dewey himself was influenced by many others; in particular he found that the card system of the Italian publisher Natale Battezzati provided "...the most fruitful source of ideas..." This just further underscores the fact that the evolution of the information science we are now practicing has been significantly iterative in its development.

CHAPTER 7

# Outlining the World and Its Parts

As we have seen, there were many early philosophers who outlined the world for informational purposes, as they saw it. While doing so is an ambitious undertaking, even for academic trailblazers, these thinkers took their studies further by constructing frameworks for information. They truly built taxonomies of the world as they saw it.

Figure 7.1: "Plato-Raphael," by Raphael.

Consider again the works of Plato, whose thoughts can be put into a hierarchical outline, his theory of knowledge displayed as an outline of knowledge. While Plato was an early outliner of reality, he was probably not the first. However, he was the first we know of who thought of the knowledge of reality as a philosophy.

The way we perceive some field, or reality in general, is our philosophy. If we look at the world through a pair of lenses, we see it one way; if we look at the world through a different pair of lenses, we see it differently. This is important to realize when you build a thesaurus, because the people involved with a particular field tend to think of the field differently from the way those outside that field might see it.

Much later than Plato, realism came along. Saint Augustine was one of the first to try to reflect the world as it really was, as he really saw it. And, perhaps inevitably for someone dealing with the nature of reality, he also did an outline of knowledge.

After Saint Augustine, another philosopher who turned thinking on its head was Saint Thomas Aquinas. He came up with yet another outline of knowledge, saying that where the particulars (the objects of the senses and of belief) are common, the characteristics are common. Without those common characteristics, an object is not the same as some other object. Coming up with the characteristics in common, so that we can say that this is the same object as some other object, and can describe it to someone who is not in your monastery but perhaps 100 miles away, to really describe it so they know exactly what you are talking or writing about, is not easy! It helps if you can group things together based on their particulars. This was really radical thinking in 1200 AD.

The outlines of knowledge that these early philosophers formulated have shaped our thoughts in the Western world and our comprehension of reality.

# CHAPTER 8

# Facets: An Indian Mathematician and Children's Toys at Selfridge's

Continuing on the efforts to build frameworks of information, a new character in this drama enters the stage by proposing an organized scheme to add important details to concepts in "facets."

Figure 8.1: Shiyali Ramamrita Ranganathan.

Shiyali Ramamrita Ranganathan (1892–1972) is known as a professor of librarianship. His academic training and early work was in mathematics, in which he earned two degrees. He taught mathematics and wrote several articles on the history of mathematics. These articles worked to his advantage when, in 1923, the University of Madras sought someone with a research background to fill the post of University Librarian. Ranganathan applied because the job paid better than his professorship at the same university. Ranganathan lacked any background in librarianship, so a few days before the job interview, he read up on the subject in the Encyclopædia Britannica! Shiyali Ranganathan got the job, but he found that it offered little intellectual stimulation and professional interaction with fellow students and colleagues. In short, the new librarian was bored, and he decided to ask to return to his prior position as a mathematics professor. He was a good thinker and both organizations wanted to keep him. The administrators agreed he would be allowed to choose which position to stay with after returning from his librarianship studies in England. After nine months of study, Ranganathan received an honors certificate from the University College London. His mathematical training gave him a unique perspective on the problems of classification and other library matters; he returned to his library position eager to put his ideas into practice.

What happened next (well, actually, in 1924), as described by noted information scientist Eugene Garfield, was pure inspiration::

> *"As so often happens in scientific discovery, this vague notion was fully conceptualized only with the help of an unlikely catalyst. For Isaac Newton, according to legend, the catalyst was a falling apple. For Friedrich Kekulé, discoverer of the benzene ring, it was a snake with a tail in its mouth that appeared to him in a dream. For Ranganathan, it was a toy erector set at Selfridge's, the London department store. There he saw a salesperson create an entirely new toy with each new combination of metal strips, nuts, and bolts. These experiences made Ranganathan realize that his classification scheme should likewise consist of elements that could be freely combined to meet the needs of each specific subject."* [14]

During his time in England, Ranganathan visited over 100 libraries to observe their operations. His observations of their shortcomings, coupled with the overall superiority of English library methods over those of India, led him to develop some egalitarian principles, published in 1931 as *The Five Laws of Library Science.* They read as follows:

- books are for use,

- every reader his book,

- every book its reader,

- save the time of the reader, and

- a library is a growing organism.

In the five laws, we can see Ranganathan's dedication to the ideal of information access for everyone. This interest dovetailed with his work in classification science. Ranganathan perceived that existing classification systems were not entirely suited to accommodating new areas of knowledge; he knew that a new, flexible approach was needed.

Figure 8.2: "Isaac Newton statue," by Andrew Gray: own work.

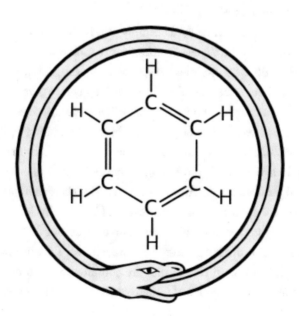

Figure 8.3: "Benzene Ouroboros," by DMGualtieri (own work).

Figure 8.4: Meccano box.

Thanks, in part, to Meccano toys [15], Ranganathan is regarded these days by many as the father of library classification science.

The classification system that Ranganathan devised, known as Colon Classification (CC), was never widely adopted. However, the theory behind it had enormous impact on classification and indexing science. According to Garfield's second essay on the famed librarian, "*Ranganathan is to library science what Einstein is to physics*" [16].

What was it that Ranganathan devised? Simply put, each *concept* or *facet* of an item can be separately detailed and assembled into a classification for that object. In the way that some personality tests classify people's traits along various "axes" or aspects, Ranganathan's system allowed all the different perspectives of an item to be classified. This was long before computers (other than simple calculators), and he wanted a shorthand notation that others would recognize by simply looking at the faceted notation he presented for a concept or an object. In a library, a physical object can only be stored in a single place. In computers now, we can have pointers from many places, but, in Ranganathan's time, the options were much more limited. He called his system the analytico-synthetic classification system and published a description of it in 1933. Ranganathan separated each of the values using a colon, hence the name colon classification. His was also known as a faceted classification system, due to the separation of each concept into a specific code and colon separated value.

The Ranganathan system of classification has evolved over six editions since its publication. The colon classification uses 42 main classes that are combined with other letters, numbers, and marks in a manner resembling the Library of Congress Classification to sort a publication.

## 8.1 RANGANATHAN'S FACETS

CC uses five primary categories, or facets, to further specify the sorting of a publication. Collectively, they are called PMEST:

1. Personality

2. Matter or property

3. Energy

4. Space

5. Time

## 8.2 RANGANATHAN'S CLASSES

The following are the main classes of CC, with some subclasses, the main method used to sort the subclass using the PMEST scheme and examples showing application of PMEST.

- z Generalia
- 1 Universe of Knowledge
- 2 Library science
- 3 Book science
- 4 Journalism
  - ∘ B Mathematics
    - B2 Algebra
  - ∘ C Physics
  - ∘ D Engineering
  - ∘ E Chemistry
  - ∘ F Technology
  - ∘ G Biology
  - ∘ H Geology
    - HX Mining
  - ∘ I Botany
  - ∘ J Agriculture
    - J1 Horticulture

- J2 Feed
- J3 Food
- J4 Stimulant
- J5 Oil
- J6 Drug
- J7 Fabric
- J8 Dye
  - K Zoology
    - KZ Animal Husbandry
  - L Medicine
    - LZ3 Pharmacology
    - LZ5 Pharmacopoeia
  - M Useful arts
    - M7 Textiles [material]:[work]
- Spiritual experience and mysticism [religion],[entity]:[problem]
  - vi. N Fine arts
    - ND Sculpture
    - NN Engraving
    - NQ Painting
    - NR Music
- Literature
  - P Linguistics
  - Q Religion
  - R Philosophy
  - S Psychology
  - T Education
  - U Geography
  - V History
  - W Political science
  - X Economics

- ◦ Y Sociology

- ◦ Z Law

A title commonly used to demonstrate the colon classification is: "Research in the cure of the tuberculosis of lungs by X-ray conducted in India in 1950s:"

- Main classification is Medicine (Medicine)

- Within Medicine, the Lungs are the main concern (Medicine,Lungs)

- The property of the Lungs is that they are afflicted with Tuberculosis (Medicine,Lungs;Tuberculosis)

- The Tuberculosis is being performed (:) on, that is the intent is to cure (Treatment) (Medicine,Lungs;Tuberculosis:Treatment)

- The matter that we are treating the Tuberculosis with are X-Rays (Medicine,Lungs;Tuberculosis:Treatment;X-ray)

- And this discussion of treatment is regarding the Research phase (Medicine,Lungs;Tuberculosis:Treatment;X-ray:Research)

- This Research is performed within a geographical space (.) namely India (Medicine,Lungs;Tuberculosis:Treatment;X-ray:Research.India)

- During the time (') of 1950 (Medicine,Lungs;Tuberculosis:Treatment;X-ray:Research.India'1950)

- Translating into the codes listed for each subject and facet the classification becomes L,45;421:6;253:f.44'N5

The components of this call number represent the following concepts as shown above but differently stated.

- L45 Medicine,Lungs;

- 421 = Tuberculosis:

- 6 = Treatment;

- 253 = X-ray:

- F = Research.

- 44'N5 = India'1950

## 8.3    A DETOUR: THESAURI IN VERSE

.. Amarakosha or Namalinganushasanam, Thesaurus Chapter 1 ..

॥ अमरकोश एवं नामलिङ्गाऽनुशासनं काण्ड १ ॥

श्री: ॥

नामलिङ्गानुशासनं नाम अमरकोष: ।

प्रथमं काण्डम् ।

मङ्गलाचरणम् ।

(१.०.१)  यस्य ज्ञानदयासिंधोरगाधस्यानघा गुणा:    mark    मङ्गलाचरणम् ॥
(१.०.२)  सेव्यतामक्षयो धीरा: स श्रिये चामृताय च
                प्रस्तावना ।

(१.०.३)  समाहृत्यान्यतन्त्राणि संक्षिप्तै: प्रतिसंस्कृतै:    mark    चिकीर्षितप्रतिज्ञा ।
(१.०.४)  संपूर्णमुच्यते वर्गैर्नामलिङ्गानुशासनम्
                परिभाषा ।

(१.०.५)  प्रायशो रूपभेदेन साहचर्याच्च कुत्रचित्    mark    परिभाषा ।
(१.०.६)  स्त्रीपुंनपुंसकं ज्ञेयं तद्विशेषविधे: क्वचित्
(१.०.७)  भेदाख्यानाय न द्वन्द्वो नैकशेषो न संकर:
(१.०.८)  कृतोऽत्र भिन्नलिङ्गानामनुक्तानां क्रमाद्व्रते
(१.०.९)  त्रिलिङ्ग्यां त्रिश्चिति पदं मिथुने तु द्वयोरिति
(१.०.१०) निषिद्धलिङ्गं शेषार्थं त्वन्ताथादि न पूर्वभाक्

स्वर्गवर्ग: ।

Heaven 9
(१.१.११)  स्वरव्ययं स्वर्गनाकत्रिदिवत्रिदशालया:    mark    अथ स्वर्गवर्ग: ।
(१.१.१२)  सुरलोको द्योदिवौ द्वे स्त्रियां क्लीबे त्रिविष्टपम्
Deities 26
(१.१.१३)  अमरा निर्जरा देवास्त्रिदशा विबुधा: सुरा:
(१.१.१४)  सुपर्वाण: सुमनसस्त्रिदिवेशा दिवौकस:
(१.१.१५)  आदितेया दिविषदो लेखा अदितिनन्दना:

१

Figure 8.5: Amarakosha.

Ranganathan may have had a predisposition toward thinking in terms of taxonomies. In his youth he may have, as schoolchildren in India still do today, learned the *Amarakosha* [17].

Just as taxonomy has evolved, so has the thesaurus, with roots dating back to about 375 AD. We know of one Sanskrit thesaurus, the *Amarakosha*, whose title translates as the "Treasury or Dictionary of Amara," written by Buddhist scholar and Sanskrit grammarian Amarasimha or Amara Simha. Interestingly, Amara Simha wrote his thesaurus in verse.

Reportedly, the ancient *Amarakosha* was almost lost to posterity. As the story goes, Amara heard of a highly respected philosopher who was traveling in the area, who wanted to engage in debate with him. Amara was afraid, and he tried to burn his manuscripts to avoid the other philosopher's scrutiny. Fortunately, the arriving visitor snatched Amara's smoking thesaurus from the flames before it was destroyed. Now, Indian school children learn to recite the verses of the *Amarakosha* from memory, and Sanskrit scholars still study the text.

The only other terminologies in verse that this author is aware of are "The Lama," by Ogden Nash, and the *Do-Re-Mi* song from *The Sound of Music*, but I don't think they bear comparison to the *Amarakosha*. In fact, author Douglas Adams complained that *Do-Re-Mi* is missing a definition, which indeed it is! (Refer to *The Salmon of Doubt: Hitchhiking the Galaxy One Last Time*, Random House, 2005, pages 34–35). But I digress...

Much more recently, and not without parallels to *Amarakosha* in the wonderfully aesthetic quality of the wording, we inevitably encounter *Roget's Thesaurus*, written in 1805. First published in 1852, as the *Thesaurus of English Words and Phrases*, its full-length title was *Thesaurus of English Words and Phrases Classified and Arranged so as to Facilitate the Expression of Ideas and Assist in Literary Composition*. The author behind this sizable vocabulary-enriching accomplishment was Peter Mark Roget (1779–1869), a British physician. As it happens, the good doctor battled periodic moods of depression by creating lists, thereby leading to the ultimate list product—his inventive and very famous thesaurus.

Figure 8.6: Peter Mark Roget, by Ernest Edwards.

*Roget's Thesaurus* is still updated and published on a frequent basis, and it is widely exploited by writers. *Roget's Thesaurus* is hierarchical to several levels, and may accurately be viewed as a complete classification system. In fact, according to its own Wikipedia page: "*The Wikipedia.org 'category schemes' … are based on the classification system in* Roget's Thesaurus, *as evidenced by the outline from the 1911 U.S. edition.*" This hierarchical quality places Roget's work in the tradition of classification systems that are also true thesauri. Associations with Roget are so predominant that in common usage the term "thesaurus" now represents a taxonomy containing relevant synonyms (plus other annotations and relationships).

However, rather than it being employed as a classification instrument, the purpose to which *Roget's Thesaurus* is most often put, and for which it is best known, is to function as a *reference synonymy*, or, in modern taxonomy parlance, a set of *synonym rings*. Roget's book presents a massive vocabulary of English word names, each term with its near-relations—and sorts every near-equivalent synonym term by the aspect of *meaning expressed* when that specific term is selected. This user-friendly structure, applied consistently from cover to cover, gives readers referring to *Roget's Thesaurus* the power to rapidly find, evaluate, and choose new phrasing to express the meaning they have in mind.

Associations with Roget are so predominant in taxonomy discussions that in this book, we will be using the terms taxonomy and thesaurus interchangeably, although they are clearly not exactly the same thing.

CHAPTER 9

# Points of Knowledge

Because we are all taxonomists by nature, to one degree or another, we follow a distinguished line of thinkers. To deal with a large body of knowledge, we need to localize and organize it. Where that knowledge is located, or where and how it is organized, or the system by which it is identified and perhaps indexed—any or all of these might be called the "points of knowledge." And certainly, databases connected to and/or indexed with knowledge organization systems represent points of knowledge.

In business terminology, points of knowledge are generally the people who have all the know-how in a particular area. If we take Biblical scripture contextually, Eve was the first being on Earth who could be considered a point of knowledge, after she started chomping on that apple (or pomegranate, or whatever the forbidden fruit was).

But maybe not. Might the first point of knowledge have been the first creature with a brain? Or before that, the first creature with biochemically dictated reflexes of some sort? These questions could take us back to the philosophic and theologic debates conducted by those mentioned earlier in this chapter, and we could spend lifetimes discussing them.

And back to speaking of apples for a moment—was Isaac Newton a single point of knowledge, after he realized what was happening to that one apple, and before he told anyone else?

Might we look at the entity of science as a whole as a single point of knowledge? Talk about a moving target, what with the frequent discoveries, and with theories proved and disproved! But classification systems, taxonomies, and thesauri that cover scientific topics, or science as a whole (as some of them try to do) could be considered single points of knowledge. For our purposes, flexibility is the key.

We've looked at some knowledge organization systems that could be considered single points of knowledge: the Linnaean taxonomy of organisms, Locke's system of knowledge (a point of knowledge of knowledge!), and the Dewey Decimal Classification, among others.

Then there are multiple points of knowledge, where several fields come together. Taxonomists and thesaurus editors frequently encounter this situation, and the accompanying challenge. It occurs most frequently with top terms (whose branches could be considered single points of knowledge), where several more specific fields come together and sometimes overlap. Should they be captured separately or together? With facets or different views? (Facets, as described by Ranganathan in his facet theory, provide multiple points of knowledge.)

Here's a very simple example: Physical biochemistry. Thank goodness for polyhierarchy, with which we can place the topic under more than one broader term (Physical chemistry; Biochemistry). But computer processing is what lets us do polyhierarchy. If we have only one copy of a physical book (remember when we didn't have to specify "physical" for a book?) on physical biochemistry, where do we shelve it?

Librarians and information specialists get to view anarchy in the universe more often than other people do—and we are the ones who have the task of taking that anarchy, or chaos, and attempting to organize the universe into some sort of order, with a thousand points of knowledge.

Perhaps it helps to think of data as independent points. Data, when organized or contextualized, becomes Information. When information becomes meaningful, it is referred to as knowledge. **Knowledge, when personalized and applied to life circumstances, becomes wisdom.**

# Glossary

**AACR, AACR2**

See Anglo-American Cataloguing Rules.

**Accuracy (in search results)**

The quality of search results, as measured by any of a variety of metrics or determined by subjective factors.

**All-and-some rule, All-and-some test**

A method for evaluating the validity of broader term–narrower term relationships. *Some* of whatever a broader term represents should be represented by each of its narrower terms, and *all* of what a narrower term represents should fit within the concept represented by a broader term.

***Amarakosha* (also *Namalinganushasana*)**

An ancient Indian thesaurus written in Sanskrit. It reportedly served as an inspiration for *Roget's Thesaurus.*

**American National Standards Institute (ANSI)**

The official standards organization for the United States.

**Anglo-American Cataloguing Rules (AACR, AACR2)**

A set of guidelines (or the publication containing those guidelines) used by library catalogers as their style guide. It has been published jointly by the American Library Association, the Canadian Library Association, and the UK's Chartered Institute of Library and Information Professionals. In 2010, AACR2 (the 2nd edition of AACR) was superseded by the Resource Description and Access (RDA) cataloging standard.

**ANSI/NISO Z39.19 (Z39.19)**

An American National Standard developed by the National Information Standards Organization (NISO), and approved July 25, 2005, by the American National Standards Institute (ANSI). Establishes a basic vocabulary for the theory and application of terminology work. It was reaffirmed in 2010 without revision as ANSI/NISO Z39.19-2005 (R2010), and is known by a variety of designations similar to that one. The full title is *Guidelines for the Construction, Format, and Management of Monolingual Controlled Vocabularies.* The 2010 version is referred to in this book as Z39.19-2010R.

**Ant colony optimization (ACO)**

An algorithmic approach to task optimization based on the behavior of ants. The probability that an ant will choose a particular path is proportional to the number of times that other ants have already chosen that path, creating a positive feedback loop. ACO algorithms are being developed and researched for a wide variety of task optimization problems, including data classification.

**API (Application programming interface)**

Programming code that a computer system provides for supporting requests made of that system by a computer program. Often used to refer to the software that implements an API.

**Associative relationship**

As defined in ANSI/NISO Z39.19-2010R, "*A relationship between or among terms in a controlled vocabulary that leads from one term to other terms that are related to or associated with it.*" A pair of terms that have an associative relationships are known as related terms; this relationship is often indicated by the acronym "RT."

**Author submission system, Submission management system**

An online platform on which authors can submit articles and associated information directly to a publisher (usually of an online article database). Often, this same platform can also be used by the editorial staff to manage peer review, internal and author review of the draft and proposed changes, and other workflow aspects of the publication process.

**Authority file, Authority list**

As defined in ANSI/NISO Z39.19-2010R, "*A set of established headings and the cross-references to be made to and from each heading, often citing the authority for the preferred form or variants. Types of authority files include name authority files and subject authority files.*"

**Auto-categorization, Auto-Indexing**

Computer-automated subject indexing.

**Auto-completion**

In search interfaces, a feature that produces a display of possible search words or phrases, sometimes based on an associated taxonomy or thesaurus, when a user starts typing a search string. In Google and similar search platforms, the completion is based on previous queries.

**Bayes' Theorem**

A major statistical principle, involving the calculation of probability based on prior statistical evidence.

**Bayesian search**

In information retrieval, the use of probability calculation methods based on Bayes' theorem to determine the likelihood of potential information resources being relevant to specific searches.

**Binomial nomenclature (Binominal nomenclature, Binary nomenclature)**

The standard system used by biologists for designating biological organisms with two-word Latin or pseudo-Latin names. The first word indicates the genus to which an organism is assumed to belong, and the second word indicates the appropriate species name within that genus.

**Boolean algebra, Boolean logic**

A form of algebra in which logical expressions contain one or more Boolean operators (AND, OR, NOT) to define sets.

**Boolean search**

A type of information search that uses the operators of Boolean logic (AND, OR, NOT), in combination with two or more search strings, to filter search results.

**Bottom-up approach (in controlled vocabulary construction)**

As explained in ANSI/NISO Z39.19-2010R, "*the necessary hierarchical structures and relationships are created as the work proceeds, but starting from the terms having the narrowest scope and moving to the more generic ones.*"

**British Standards Institution, BSI (aka BSI Group)**

The organization officially recognized by the government of the United Kingdom as the UK's National Standards Body. BSI is the UK member of the international standards organizations, ISO and IEC.

**Broader term**

As defined in ANSI/NISO Z39.19-2010R, "*A term to which another term or multiple terms are subordinate in a hierarchy. In thesauri, the relationship indicator for this type of term is BT.*"

**Browsing**

As defined in ANSI/NISO Z39.19-2010R, "*The process of visually scanning through organized collections of representations of content objects, controlled vocabulary terms, hierarchies, taxonomies, thesauri, etc.*"

**Candidate term**

As defined in ANSI/NISO Z39.19-2010R, "*A term under consideration for admission into a controlled vocabulary because of its potential usefulness.*"

**Classification scheme**

As defined in ANSI/NISO Z39.19-2010R, "*A method of organization according to a set of pre-established principles, usually characterized by a notation system and a hierarchical structure of relationships among the entities.*"

**Collabulary**

As defined by Jonathon Keats, *"A collaborative vocabulary for tagging Web content. Like the folksonomies used on social bookmarking sites like del.icio.us [now Delicious], collabularies are generated by a community. But unlike folksonomies, they're automatically vetted for consistency, extracting the wisdom of crowds from the cacophony."* (Jonathon Keats, "Jargon Watch," *Wired*, January 1, 2007)

**Colon classification**

A library classification system developed by S.R. Ranganathan. It is reputed to be the first faceted classification system.

**Compound term**

As defined in ANSI/NISO Z39.19-2010R, *"A term consisting of more than one word that represents a single concept."*

**Controlled vocabulary**

As defined in ANSI/NISO Z39.19-2010R:

*"A list of terms that have been enumerated explicitly. This list is controlled by and is available from a controlled vocabulary registration authority. All terms in a controlled vocabulary must have an unambiguous, non-redundant definition. NOTE: This is a design goal that may not be true in practice; it depends on how strict the controlled vocabulary registration authority is regarding registration of terms into a controlled vocabulary.*

*"At a minimum, the following two rules must be enforced:*

*"1. If the same term is commonly used to mean different concepts, then its name is explicitly qualified to resolve this ambiguity. NOTE: This rule does not apply to synonym rings.*

*"2. If multiple terms are used to mean the same thing, one of the terms is identified as the preferred term in the controlled vocabulary and the other terms are listed as synonyms or aliases."*

"Registration authority" refers to any taxonomy editor or taxonomy team that has some sort of authorization for control of the vocabulary, or the organization granting them the authority, will serve the purpose.

## COSATI

The Federal Council on Science and Technology's Committee on Scientific and Technical Information. It was operational from the early 1960s to the early 1970s.

**Cutter Expansive Classification** (often referred to as **Cutter classification**)

A library classification system developed by Charles Ammi Cutter in the 1880s. It serves as the basis for the Library of Congress Classification.

**Data visualization**

The use of a graphical visual representation to convey or interpret data.

**DCMI**

See Dublin Core Metadata Initiative.

**Descriptor**

See Preferred term.

**Dewey Decimal Classification (**commonly known as the **Dewey Decimal System)**

A library classification system developed by Melvil Dewey in the 1870s and 1880s. It formed the basis of the Universal Decimal Classification.

**Dublin Core, Dublin Core Metadata Element Set**

As described by the Dublin Core Metadata Initiative at http://dublincore.org/documents/dces/, "*The Dublin Core Metadata Element Set is a vocabulary of fifteen properties for use in resource description. The name 'Dublin' is due to its origin at a 1995 invitational workshop in Dublin, Ohio; 'core' because its elements are broad and generic, usable for describing a wide range of resources.*" This core metadata element set is usually referred to as "Dublin Core."

**Dublin Core Metadata Initiative (DCMI)**

According to DCMI's website (http://dublincore.org/), "*The Dublin Core Metadata Initiative, or 'DCMI,' is an open organization supporting innovation in metadata design and best practices across the metadata ecology. DCMI's activities include work on architecture and modeling, discussions and collaborative work in DCMI Communities and DCMI Task Groups, global conferences, meetings and workshops, and educational efforts to promote widespread acceptance of metadata standards and best practices.*" DCMI is the main promulgator of the Dublin Core metadata standards.

**Editorial note**

A note connected with a controlled vocabulary term (usually in a designated field in the term record), for the purpose of communicating information having to do with in-house editorial and vocabulary development matters. Editorial notes are generally not exposed to Internet display.

**Enterprise software**

Software designed for use by several people simultaneously within an organization.

**Entry term, Non-preferred term**

A synonym or quasi-synonym for a preferred term. Non-preferred terms are not used for indexing, but can direct a manual indexer or an automated indexing system to use the corresponding preferred terms. "Entry terms" (but not "non-preferred terms") may also be considered to include indexing terms.

**Epistemology, Theory of knowledge**

The philosophical field covering the study of the nature of knowledge.

**Equivalence relationship**

> As defined in ANSI/NISO Z39.19-2010R, *"A relationship between or among terms in a controlled vocabulary that leads to one or more terms that are to be used instead of the term from which the cross-reference is made."*

**Faceted classification, Faceted taxonomy**

> A method of taxonomic classification in which terms or subjects are placed in a variety of mutually exclusive categories (such as color or location), in order to reflect various aspects or dimensions of each subject.

**Faceted search, Fielded search**

> Search of information organized or indexed according to a faceted classification system, allowing multiple filters for narrowing of the search according to variety of dimensions or aspects. Often used in e-commerce.

**Hierarchical relationship**

> As defined in ANSI/NISO Z39.19-2010R, *"A relationship between or among terms in a controlled vocabulary that depicts broader (generic) to narrower (specific) or whole–part relationships; begins with the words broader term (BT), or narrower term (NT)."*

**Hierarchy**

> As defined in ANSI/NISO Z39.19-2010R, *"Broader (generic) to narrower (specific) or whole–part relationships, which are generally indicated in a controlled vocabulary through codes or indentation."*

**Homograph**

> As defined in ANSI/NISO Z39.19-2010R: *"One of two or more words that have the same spelling, but different meanings and origins. In controlled vocabularies, homographs are generally distinguished by qualifiers."* I discourage the use of qualifiers, and encourage the use of other means whenever possible to differentiate homograms (homographs).

**Indexing**

> As defined in ANSI/NISO Z39.19-2010R, *"A method by which terms or subject headings from a controlled vocabulary are selected by a human or computer to represent the concepts in or attributes of a content object. The terms may or may not occur in the content object."* This kind of indexing should not be confused with indexing processes for creating a book index or a data index.

**Indexing term**

> As defined in ANSI/NISO Z39.19-2010R, *"The representation of a concept in an indexing language, generally in the form of a noun or noun phrase. Terms, subject headings, and heading-subheading combinations are examples of indexing terms. Also called descriptor."*

**Keyword**

As defined in ANSI/NISO Z39.19-2010R, "*A word occurring in the natural language of a document that is considered significant for indexing and retrieval.*" Keywords can be assigned to a work by its author(s), or can be words used in search queries.

**LCSH**

See *Library of Congress Subject Headings.*

**Library of Congress Classification**

The system of library classification developed and maintained by the Library of Congress. It is used by many university and research libraries, as well as by the Library of Congress, for classifying library holdings.

**Library of Congress Subject Headings (LCSH)**

A thesaurus of subject headings maintained and used by the Library of Congress for subject metadata in library catalog records.

**Linked data**

Structured data that is connected with other data resources, based on some relationships considered to be useful, with each piece of data identified by an http URI.

**Literary warrant (See also User warrant, Organizational warrant)**

As defined in ANSI/NISO Z39.19-2010R, "*Justification for the representation of a concept in an indexing language or for the selection of a preferred term because of its frequent occurrence in the literature.*"

**MARC (Machine-Readable Cataloging)**

A set of digital formats for the bibliographic description of library holdings, developed by the Library of Congress and now an international standard.

**Machine-assisted indexing**

Indexing using software that suggests indexing terms from one or more controlled vocabularies, but that allows a human indexer to make the final determination as to which terms will be used for indexing of each resource.

**MeSH (Medical Subject Headings)**

A thesaurus of subject headings developed and maintained by the U.S. National Library of Medicine (NLM), and used by NLM for cataloging MEDLINE and PubMed articles.

**Metadata**

There are many kinds of metadata. Metadata is data about data—it provides the overview of an item. This book mostly refers to subject metadata from a thesaurus but descriptive metadata is the most common usage. Descriptive metadata is used to provide descriptive information about information resources. In bibliographic records and similar metadata records, the terms for the subject metadata record fields are typically obtained from a taxonomy, thesaurus, or similar classification scheme. In addition to subject and descriptive metadata, records can contain structural metadata and administrative metadata.

**Narrower term**

As defined in ANSI/NISO Z39.19-2010R, "*A term that is subordinate to another term or to multiple terms in a hierarchy. In thesauri, the relationship indicator for this type of term is NT.*"

**National Information Standards Organization (NISO)**

As NISO describes itself at http://www.niso.org/about/, "*NISO, the National Information Standards Organization, a non-profit association accredited by the American National Standards Institute (ANSI), identifies, develops, maintains, and publishes technical standards to manage information in our changing and ever-more digital environment. NISO standards apply both traditional and new technologies to the full range of information-related needs, including retrieval, re-purposing, storage, metadata, and preservation.*"

**Natural language**

As defined in ANSI/NISO Z39.19-2010R, "*A language used by human beings for verbal communication. Words extracted from natural language texts for indexing purposes without vocabulary control are often called keywords.*"

**Natural language processing (NLP)**

Computer processing of text presented in natural language.

**Navigation (**See also **Browsing)**

As defined in ANSI/NISO Z39.19-2010R, "*The process of moving through a controlled vocabulary or an information space via some pre-established links or relationships. For example, navigation in a controlled vocabulary could mean moving from a broader term to one or more narrower terms using the predefined relationships.*"

**NISO, National Information Standards Organization**

As NISO describes itself at http://www.niso.org/about/, "*NISO, the National Information Standards Organization, a non-profit association accredited by the American National Standards Institute (ANSI), identifies, develops, maintains, and publishes technical standards to manage information in our changing and ever-more digital environment. NISO standards apply both traditional and new technologies to the full range of information-related needs, including retrieval, re-purposing, storage, metadata, and preservation.*"

**NLP**

See *Natural language processing*

**Node label**

As defined in ANSI/NISO Z39.19-2010R, "*A 'dummy' term, often a phrase, that is not assigned to documents when indexing, but which is inserted into the hierarchical section of some controlled vocabularies to indicate the logical basis on which a class has been divided. Node labels may also be used to group categories of related terms in the alphabetic section of a controlled vocabulary."*

**Non-preferred term, Entry term**

A synonym or quasi-synonym for a preferred term. Non-preferred terms are not used for indexing, but can direct a manual indexer or an automated indexing system to use the corresponding preferred terms. "Entry terms" (but not "non-preferred terms") may also be considered to include indexing terms.

**ONIX (Online Information eXchange)**

As described by EDitEUR, one of several organizations involved in the development of ONIX, *"an XML-based family of international standards intended to support computer-to-computer communication between parties involved in creating, distributing, licensing or otherwise making available intellectual property in published form, whether physical or digital."*

**Ontology**

As explained by the World Wide Web Consortium (W3C) at http://www.w3.org/standards/semanticweb/ontology, *"There is no clear division between what is referred to as 'vocabularies' and 'ontologies.' The trend is to use the word 'ontology' for more complex, and possibly quite formal collection of terms, whereas 'vocabulary' is used when such strict formalism is not necessarily used or only in a very loose sense."*

**Organizational warrant** (See also **User warrant, Literary warrant**)

As defined in ANSI/NISO Z39.19-2010R, *"Justification for the representation of a concept in an indexing language or for the selection of a preferred term due to characteristics and context of the organization."*

**OWL (Web Ontology Language)**

An XML-based format designed by the World Wide Web Consortium (W3C) for use in ontologies. As described by W3C at http://www.w3.org/standards/techs/owl#w3c_all, *"The OWL Web Ontology Language is designed for use by applications that need to process the content of information instead of just presenting information to humans. OWL facilitates greater machine interpretability of Web content than that supported by XML, RDF, and RDF Schema (RDF-S) by providing additional vocabulary along with a formal semantics. OWL has three increasingly-expressive sublanguages: OWL Lite, OWL DL, and OWL Full."*

**Permuted display**

As defined in Z39.19, *"A type of index where individual words of a term are rotated to bring each word of the term into alphabetical order in the term list."*

**Polyhierarchy**

The property of a taxonomy or thesaurus whereby a term can exist in more than one place in the overall hierarchical structure, having multiple broader terms.

**Post-coordination**

As defined in ANSI/NISO Z39.19-2010R, "*The combining of terms at the searching stage rather than at the subject heading list construction stage or indexing stage.*"

**Pre-coordination**

As defined in ANSI/NISO Z39.19-2010R, "*The formulation of a multiword heading or the linking of a heading and subheadings to create a formally controlled, multi-element expression of a concept or object.*"

**Precision (in search results)**

As defined in ANSI/NISO Z39.19-2010R, "*A measure of a search system's ability to retrieve only relevant content objects. Usually expressed as a percentage calculated by dividing the number of retrieved relevant content objects by the total number of content objects retrieved.*"

**Preferred term**

As defined in ANSI/NISO Z39.19-2010R, "*One of two or more synonyms or lexical variants selected as a term for inclusion in a controlled vocabulary.*"

**Provisional term**

See *Candidate term.*

**RDA (Resource Description and Access)**

A set of guidelines published jointly in 2010 by the American Library Association, the Canadian Library Association, and the UK's Chartered Institute of Library and Information Professionals, and intended to replace the *Anglo-American Cataloguing Rules*, 2nd Edition (AACR2).

**RDF (Resource Description Framework)**

As described by the World Wide Web Consortium (W3C) at http://www.w3.org/RDF/, "*RDF is a standard model for data interchange on the Web. RDF has features that facilitate data merging even if the underlying schemas differ, and it specifically supports the evolution of schemas over time without requiring all the data consumers to be changed. RDF extends the linking structure of the Web to use URIs to name the relationship between things as well as the two ends of the link (this is usually referred to as a 'triple'). Using this simple model, it allows structured and semi-structured data to be mixed, exposed, and shared across different applications.*"

**Recall (in search results)**

As defined in ANSI/NISO Z39.19, "*A measure of a search system's ability to retrieve all relevant content objects. Usually expressed as a percentage calculated by dividing the number of retrieved relevant content objects by the number of all relevant content objects in a collection.*"

**Reciprocity (of term relationships)**

As explained in ANSI/NISO Z39.19, "*Semantic relationships in controlled vocabularies must be reciprocal, that is each relationship from one term to another must also be represented by a recip-*

*rocal relationship in the other direction. Reciprocal relationships may be symmetric, e.g. RT / RT, or asymmetric e.g., BT/NT."*

**Related term**

As defined in ANSI/NISO Z39.19, *"A term that is associatively but not hierarchically linked to another term in a controlled vocabulary."* It is intended to expand the searcher's awareness of the vocabulary, suggesting other concepts that may be of interest.

**Resource Description and Access**

See RDA.

**Scope note**

As defined in ANSI/NISO Z39.19-2010R, *"A note following a term explaining its coverage, specialized usage, or rules for assigning it."*

**Semantic Web**

As described by the World Wide Web Consortium (W3C) at http://www.w3.org/2001/sw/, *"The Semantic Web is about two things. It is about common formats for integration and combination of data drawn from diverse sources, where on the original Web mainly concentrated on the interchange of documents. It is also about language for recording how the data relates to real world objects. That allows a person, or a machine, to start off in one database, and then move through an unending set of databases which are connected not by wires but by being about the same thing."*

**SKOS (Simple Knowledge Organization System)**

According to the World Wide Web Consortium (W3C) at http://www.w3.org/TR/skos-reference/, *"a common data model for sharing and linking knowledge organization systems via the Web. Many knowledge organization systems, such as thesauri, taxonomies, classification schemes and subject heading systems, share a similar structure, and are used in similar applications. SKOS captures much of this similarity and makes it explicit, to enable data and technology sharing across diverse applications. The SKOS data model provides a standard, low-cost migration path for porting existing knowledge organization systems to the Semantic Web. SKOS also provides a lightweight, intuitive language for developing and sharing new knowledge organization systems. It may be used on its own, or in combination with formal knowledge representation languages such as the Web Ontology language (OWL)."*

**Structured data**

Data in which the text of each information resource is partitioned into fields, often delimited by XML "tags" or field labels indicating the kind of metadata element contained within each field.

**Subject heading**

As explained in ANSI/NISO Z39.19-2010R: *"A word or phrase, or any combination of words, phrases, and modifiers used to describe the topic of a content object. Precoordination of terms for multiple and related concepts is a characteristic of subject headings that distinguishes them from controlled vocabulary terms."*

**Subject matter expert (SME)**

In taxonomy and thesaurus development, a person who has deep knowledge of a subject area represented in the vocabulary, and who provides advice and feedback regarding such matters as term wording, hierarchical structure, appropriate non-preferred terms, and terms or concepts to consider adding.

**Synonym ring**

As defined in ANSI/NISO Z39.19-2010R, *"A group of terms that are considered equivalent for the purposes of retrieval."* Terms in a synonym ring are not distinguished as preferred or non-preferred.

**Taxonomy**

As defined in ANSI/NISO Z39.19-2010R, *"A collection of controlled vocabulary terms organized into a hierarchical structure. Each term in a taxonomy is in one or more parent/child (broader/narrower) relationships to other terms in the taxonomy."*

**Term**

As defined in ANSI/NISO Z39.19-2010R, *"One or more words designating a concept."*

**Terminology registry**

A descriptive catalog of terminologies, usually containing taxonomies and thesauri, as well as other kinds of controlled vocabularies.

**Theory of knowledge**

See Epistemology.

**Thesaurus (plural Thesauri or Thesauruses)**

As defined in ANSI/NISO Z39.19-2010R, *"A controlled vocabulary arranged in a known order and structured so that the various relationships among terms are displayed clearly and identified by standardized relationship indicators."*

**Top-down approach (in controlled vocabulary construction)**

As explained in ANSI/NISO Z39.19-2010R, *"The broadest terms are identified first and then narrower terms are selected to reach the desired level of specificity. The necessary hierarchical structures and relationships are created as the work proceeds."*

**Training set**

A set of documents used in developing the indexing capabilities of a statistics-based indexing system.

**Truncation**

Shortening of a word or phrase, sometimes replacing the omitted portion with a wildcard character that can represent any and all characters. This technique is used to give more comprehensive results when creating search strings or indexing rules.

**Turney's algorithm**

A semantic approach to sentiment analysis. A *"simple unsupervised learning algorithm for classifying reviews as recommended (thumbs up) or not recommended (thumbs down). The classification of a review is predicted by the average semantic orientation of the phrases in the review that contain adjectives or adverbs. A phrase has a positive semantic orientation when it has good associations (e.g., 'subtle nuances') and a negative semantic orientation when it has bad associations (e.g., 'very cavalier')"* (In Peter D. Turney, "Thumbs Up or Thumbs Down? Semantic Orientation Applied to Unsupervised Classification of Reviews," *Proceedings of the 40th Annual Meeting of the Association for Computational Linguistics*, Philadelphia, July 2002: 417–424).

**UID**

Unique identifier. An identification number or alphanumeric code often used with taxonomy and thesaurus terms, term records, and concept records.

**Unicode**

As described by Unicode, Inc., at http://www.unicode.org/standard/standard.html, *"The Unicode Standard is a character coding system designed to support the worldwide interchange, processing, and display of the written texts of the diverse languages and technical disciplines of the modern world. In addition, it supports classical and historical texts of many written languages."*

**Universal Decimal Classification (UDC)**

As described by the UDC Consortium at www.udcc.org, *"UDC is one of the most widely used classification schemes for all fields of knowledge. It is used in libraries, bibliographic, documentation and information services in over 130 countries around the world and is published in over 40 languages."*

**Unstructured text**

See *Structured text*. Unstructured text lacks such metadata labeling.

**User warrant**

As defined in ANSI/NISO Z39.19-2010R, *"Justification for the representation of a concept in an indexing language or for the selection of a preferred term because of frequent requests for information on the concept or free-text searches on the term by users of an information storage and retrieval system."*

**Vocabulary control**

As defined in ANSI/NISO Z39.19-2010R: *"The process of organizing a list of terms (a) to indicate which of two or more synonymous terms is authorized for use; (b) to distinguish between homographs; and (c) to indicate hierarchical and associative relationships among terms in the context of a controlled vocabulary or subject heading list."*

### W3C, World Wide Web Consortium

As described by W3C at http://www.w3.org/Consortium/, *"The World Wide Web Consortium (W3C) is an international community where Member organizations, a full-time staff, and the public work together to develop Web standards. Led by Web inventor Tim Berners-Lee and CEO Jeffrey Jaffe, W3C's mission is to lead the Web to its full potential."*

### Web Ontology Language (OWL)

An XML-based format designed by the World Wide Web Consortium (W3C) for use in ontologies. As described by W3C at http://www.w3.org/standards/techs/owl#w3c_all, *"The OWL Web Ontology Language is designed for use by applications that need to process the content of information instead of just presenting information to humans. OWL facilitates greater machine interpretability of Web content than that supported by XML, RDF, and RDF Schema (RDF-S) by providing additional vocabulary along with a formal semantics. OWL has three increasingly-expressive sublanguages: OWL Lite, OWL DL, and OWL Full."*

### Z39.19 (ANSI/NISO Z39.19)

Taxonomy and thesaurus standard developed by the National Information Standards Organization (NISO), and approved July 25, 2005, by the American National Standards Institute (ANSI). Establishes a basic vocabulary for the theory and application of terminology work. It was reaffirmed in 2010 without revision as ANSI/NISO Z39.19-2005 (R2010), and is known by a variety of designations similar to that one. The full title is *Guidelines for the Construction, Format, and Management of Monolingual Controlled Vocabularies.* The 2010 version is referred to in this book as Z39.19-2010R. It does not embrace the vocabulary dealing with computer applications in terminology work which was covered by withdrawn standard ISO 1087-2.

# End Notes

1   *"The Classical Period or Golden Age of Greece, from around 500 to 300 BC, has given us the great monuments, art, philosophy, architecture and literature which are the building blocks of our own civilization."* http://www.ahistoryofgreece.com/goldenage.htm.

2   Bertrand Russell, "Theory of Knowledge," Encyclopædia Britannica, 1926. Article is available online at https://www.marxists.org/reference/subject/philosophy/works/en/russell1.htm.

3   Tod F. Stuessy, *Plant Taxonomy: The Systematic Evaluation of Comparative Data*, Second Edition (Columbia University Press, 2009), p. 136. DOI: 10.2307/2806812.

4   http://www.philosophybasics.com/branch_realism.html.

5   http://www.philosophybasics.com/branch_realism.html.

6   The actual dates of William of Ockham's birth and death are unknown, as is the case with many medieval figures. Dates have been estimated based on events that occurred later in his life.

7   Paul Vincent Spade and Claude Panaccio, "William of Ockham," *The Stanford Encyclopedia of Philosophy* (Fall 2011 Edition), edited by Edward N. Zalta, http://plato.stanford.edu/archives/fall2011/entries/ockham.

8   Ockham is also credited with the principle of "***Ockham's razor**, also spelled **Occam's razor**, also called **law of economy** or **law of parsimony**. The principle gives precedence to simplicity; of two competing theories, the simpler explanation of an entity is to be preferred. The principle is also expressed as 'Entities are not to be multiplied beyond necessity.'"* Some claim, however, that the principle was first expressed by Durand de Saint-Pourçain, a French Dominican theologian and philosopher. http://www.britannica.com/EBchecked/topic/424706/Ockhams-razor.

9   David L. Block and Kenneth C. Freeman, *Shrouds of the Night: Masks of the Milky Way and Our Awesome New View of Galaxies* (Springer Science + Business Media, LLC, 2008), pp. 49–50.

10  Although Aristotle and Theophrastus both used the binomial nomenclature system, as did Carl Linneaus much later, the Gaspard brothers get the credit.

11   T. A. Sprague, "Linnaeus as Nomenclaturist," *Taxon*, 2, no. 3 (May 1953): *Linnaeus: Species Plantarum* (pp. 40–46), p 40.

12   http://en.wikipedia.org/wiki/An_Essay_Concerning_Human_Understanding.

13   http://en.wikipedia.org/wiki/Immanuel_Kant.

14   Eugene Garfield, "A Tribute to S.R. Ranganathan, the Father of Indian Library Science. Part 1. Life and Works," *Current Contents*, no. 6 (February 6, 1984), pp. 5–12. Reprinted in *Essays of an Information Scientist*, Volume 7 (Philadelphia: ISI Press, 1985), pp. 37–44.

15   Meccano model sets were produced at the time in England by Meccano, Ltd. Meccano toys are still produced today, at a facility in Calais, France, that was built by the company in 1959.

16   Eugene Garfield, "A Tribute to S.R. Ranganathan, the Father of Library Science. Part 2. Contribution to Indian and International Library Science," *Current Contents*, no. 7, (February 13, 1984) pp. 3–7. Reprinted in *Essays of an Information Scientist*, Volume 7. (Philadelphia: ISI Press, 1985, pp. 45–49.)

17   http://sanskritdocuments.org/doc_z_misc_amarakosha.html, http://sanskritdocuments.org/doc_z_misc_major_works/amarfin1.pdf.

# Author Biography

Marjorie M.K. Hlava and her team have worked with or built over 600 controlled vocabularies. Their experience is shared with you in this book. Margie is well known internationally for her work in the implementation of information science principles and the ever-evolving technology that supports them. She and the team at Access Innovations have provided the "back room" operations for many information related organizations over the last 40 years. Margie is very active in the main organizations concerned with those areas. She has served as president of NFAIS (the National Federation of Advanced Information Services); that organization awarded her the Anne Marie Cunningham Memorial Award for Exemplary Volunteer Service to the Federation in 2012, as well as the Miles Conrad lectureship in 2014. She has also served as president of the American Society for Information Science and Technology (ASIS&T), which has awarded her the prestigious Watson Davis Award. She has served two terms on the Board of Directors of the Special Libraries Association (SLA); SLA has honored her with their President's Award for her work in standards and has made her a Fellow of the SLA for her many other services within the organization. More recently, she served as the founding chair of SLA's Taxonomy Division.

For five years, Margie was on the Board of the National Information Standards Organization (NISO), and she continues to serve on the Content and Collaboration Standards Topic Committee for NISO. She has also held numerous committee positions in these and other organizations. She convened the workshop leading to the ANSI/NISO thesaurus standard NISO Z39.19-2005, and was a member of the standards committee for its writing. She also acted as liaison to the British Standards Institute controlled vocabulary standards group to ensure that the U.S. and British standards would be compatible.

Margie is the founder and president of Access Innovations, Inc., which has been honored with many awards, including recognition several times by *KMWorld Magazine* as one of 100 Companies That Matter in Knowledge Management and as a Trend-Setting Product Company, as well as by *EContent Magazine* as one of 100 Companies That Matter Most in the Digital Content Industry. The company's information management services include thesaurus and taxonomy creation. Under Margie's guidance, Access Innovations has developed the Data Harmony® line of software for content creation, taxonomy management, and automated categorization for portals and data collections. The Data Harmony Suite is protected by two patents, numbers 6898586 and 8046212, and 21 patent claims. Her recognition of the value of automatic code suggestion for the medical industry led to the founding of Access Integrity and its Medical Claims Compliance system.

Margie's primary areas of research include automated indexing, thesaurus development, taxonomy creation, natural language processing, machine translations, and computer aided indexing. She has authored more than 200 published articles on these subjects. At industry and association meetings, she has given numerous workshops and presentations on thesaurus and taxonomy creation and maintenance.